www.FlowerpotPress.com
PAB-0808-0362 · 978-1-4867-2895-4
Made in China/Fabriqué en Chine

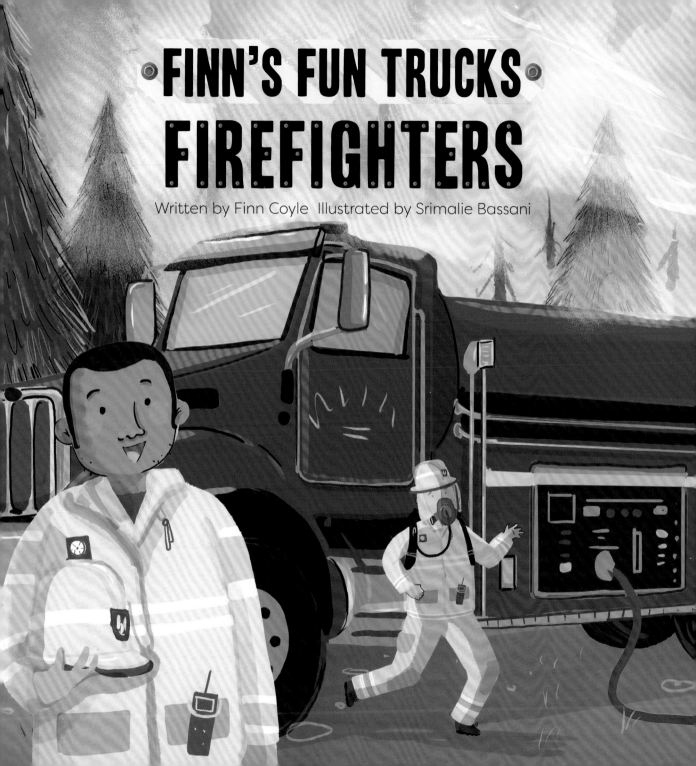

FINN'S FUN TRUCKS
FIREFIGHTERS

Written by Finn Coyle   Illustrated by Srimalie Bassani

We are firefighters. We help fight fires using some really awesome machines.

Each one has a job of its own.
Can you guess what each one does?

This is a
FIRE TRUCK.
Can you guess what it does?

AERIAL LADDER

FLOOD LIGHTS

GRIPPED STEPS

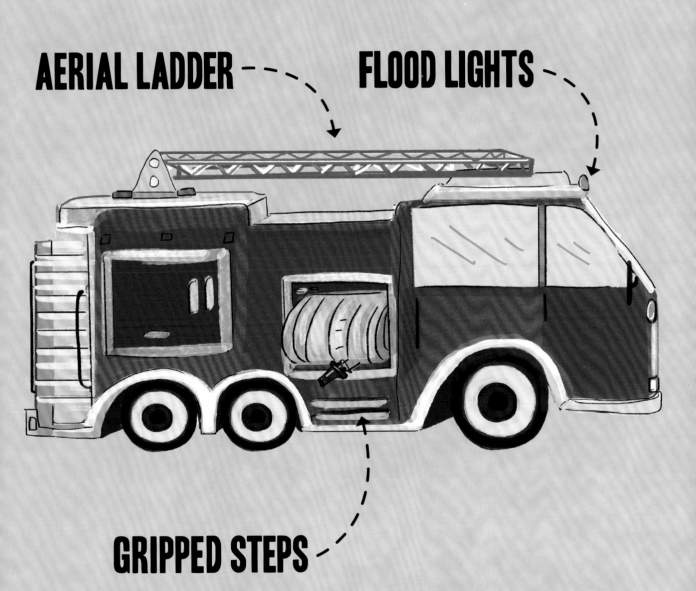

A fire truck helps firefighters put out fires. Firefighters use it as transportation, but it can also carry the equipment they need, including a hose and a ladder.

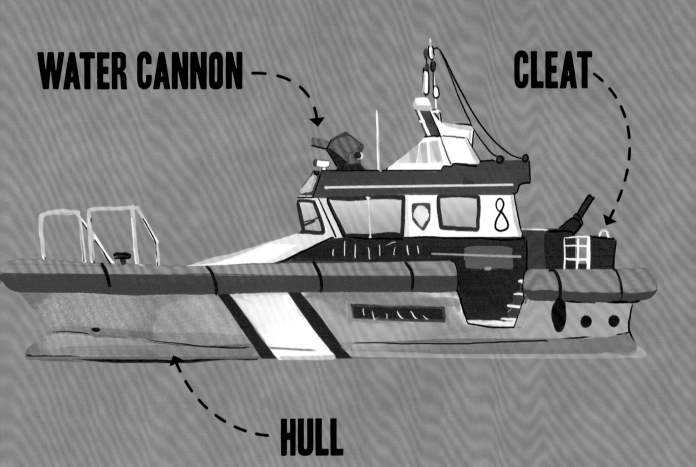

WATER CANNON

CLEAT

HULL

A fireboat helps firefighters fight fires on boats or near shorelines. It can also provide emergency response and perform rescue operations on rivers and other bodies of water.

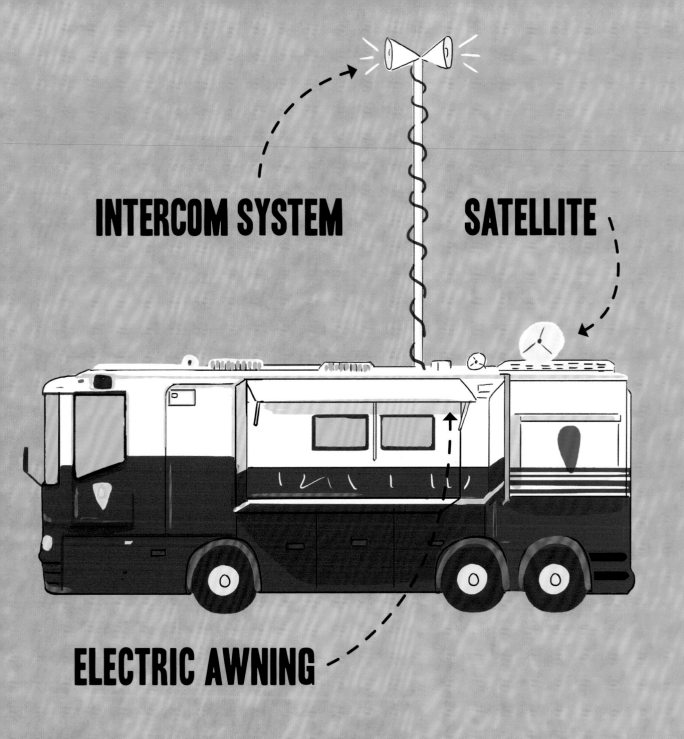

INTERCOM SYSTEM

SATELLITE

ELECTRIC AWNING

A mobile command center acts as the fire station when the fire fleet is called to a scene.

This is where firefighters can communicate with other vehicles and make important decisions on the go.

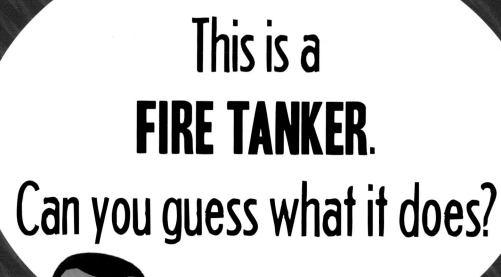

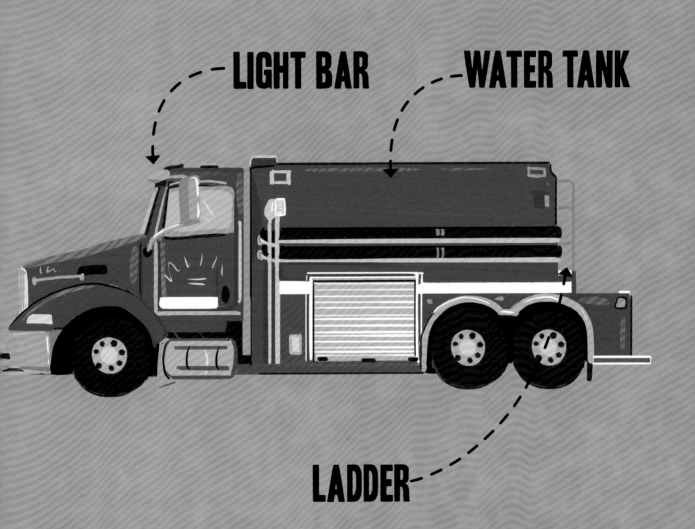

LIGHT BAR

WATER TANK

LADDER

A fire tanker is a large truck that can hold lots of water so firefighters can put out fires when hydrants cannot be used or aren't available.

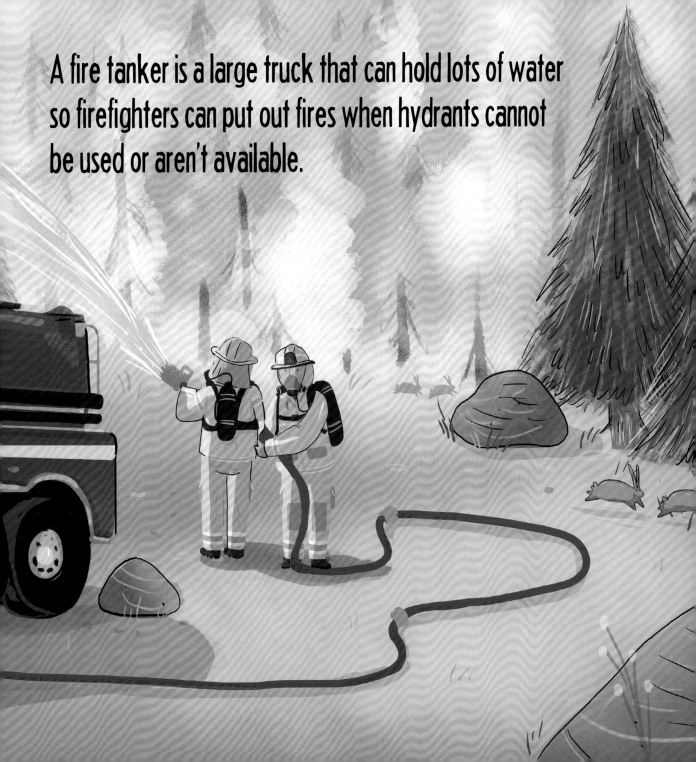

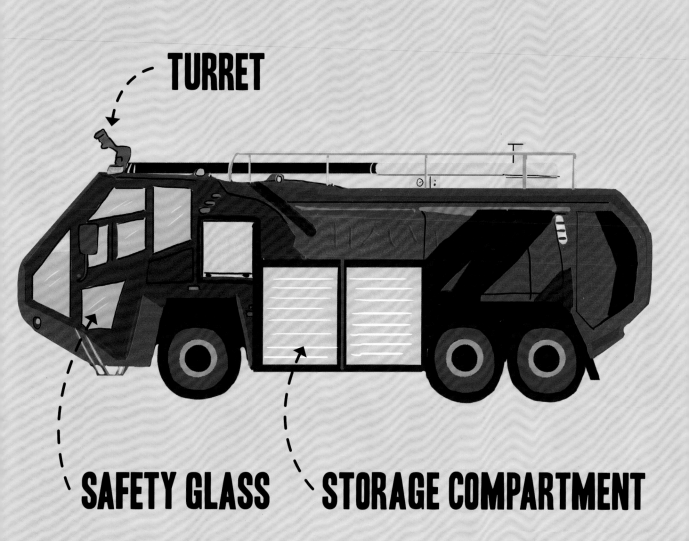

TURRET

SAFETY GLASS

STORAGE COMPARTMENT

An aircraft rescue and fire fighting vehicle (ARFF) helps fight fires at airports. It can also perform rescues for passengers and crew on airplanes in case of an emergency.

We are firefighters! Can you guess what we can do when we all work together?

We can help rescue people from fire emergencies and put out fires wherever they may be!

FIRE TRUCK

MOBILE COMMAND
CENTER

FIRE TANKER

FIREBOAT

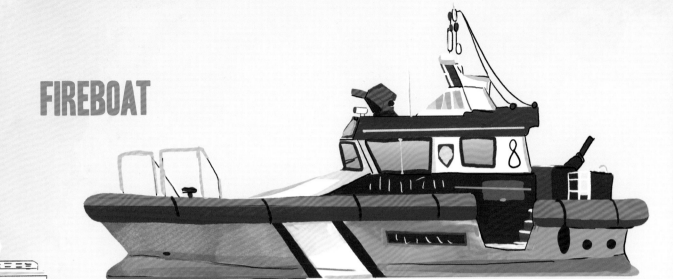

AIRCRAFT RESCUE AND
FIRE FIGHTING VEHICLE

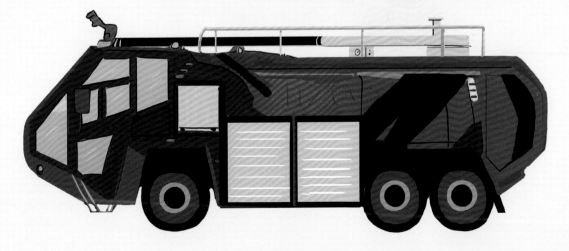